WHERE DID THE SUMMER GO?

Bil Keane

FAWCETT GOLD MEDAL • NEW YORK

A Fawcett Gold Medal Book
Published by Ballantine Books
Copyright © 1982, 1987 by Cowles Syndicate, Inc.

Library of Congress Catalog Card Number: 87-90778

ISBN 0-449-12426-6

Manufactured in the United States of America

First Edition: August 1987

10 9 8 7 6 5 4 3 2 1

"This is the best month to go on vacation 'cause August doesn't have any holidays. You hafta make your own."

"I'd like to know what happened to all the
dental floss."

"It must be tough bein' an only child. You're
outnumbered by parents."

"You'll have to buy me some new cords,
Mommy. I've worn the treads off these."

"Why don't you have them take numbers?"

"There's no lemonade, Kool-Aid or Gatorade.
Mommy says to drink waterade."

"It's so hot out there I have tears all over my body."

"I think Mommy's mad at us. We're havin' turnips."

"Mmm! This is scrumptious!"
"Can I have some scrumptious, Mommy?"

"Strike fourteen!"

"Here, Barfy, do you want this Popsicle bone?"

"I can see why frogs don't dance much."

"I stumped my daddy toe!"

"What's happened on 'All My Children' since the middle of June?"

"Daddy's washing the grass."

"If Barfy starts meowing it's 'cause he ate Kittycat's food."

"I want to cancel Dolly's ballet lessons for the next three weeks."

"When we get to the Grand Canyon you children are not to touch a thing."

"I'd feel better if we had four leashes."

"Wish they had something like this between our house and the school."

"I saw it on TV once, but it looked littler."

"It'd be easier if they had escalators."

"The ranger said the river dug the canyon,
Mommy, and you said God
did it. Who's right?"

"Why not?"

"Is this bus and the mules the only rides to go
on at the Grand Canyon?"

"After we see the sunrise, THEN can we all go
back to bed?"

"This is like a church, Mommy. Everyone's whispering."

"Stop eating 'tato chips, Jeffy. We're tryin' to hear the river."

"Gee! This is too much like SCHOOL!"

"Reminds me of that rainbow layer cake you
made for my birthday."

"Daddy's pictures will be better than these 'cause we'll be in them."

"It smells like Christmas here."

"Why does Mommy hafta be alone to medicate?"

"That's gonna be a hard act to follow."

"They have all those needles 'cause they don't like to be climbed."

"Let's try THIS motel, Daddy! They have swings out back, and color TV and a lawn and kids next door and..."

"Just this morning I was reading on the cereal
box that . . . ."

"I hear somebody coming. I'll put you on hold."

"I always bring some toys with me in case I
get boring."

"You have guilt written all over your face."

"He's looking at our speedometer."

"Are you going out for a team, Mommy?"

"I'll show you how to breathe. First you inhale, then you outhale."

"If the 'conomy doesn't get better I think
Daddy might have to let a couple of us go."

"Mommy, a feather fell off your tree."

"He's a good watchdog — between naps."

"Mmmm! Strawbabies and fream!"

"And I wasn't even allowed to keep a FROG in my room!"

"... and E.T. wanted to phone home and his
finger would glow and ... boy, Grandma!
You'd like it! ... Wanna know how
it ends? ..."

"I'm 5 and I know how to write my name!"

"Mommy! I swallowed a watermelon seed, will
a watermelon grow inside me?"

"Did you know this movie was made once before?"
"Yes, Grandma. We saw the original virgin."

"I heard a strange noise out in the garage."

"Do we need cough drops, Mommy? A pen? How 'bout razor blades? Film? Gum? . . ."

"I have to be quarterback. You've got the wrong number."

"That's a police car. You can tell by the disco lights on top."

"There's a little girl in my room who can even spell 'carpenter'. Her name is Mary Carpenter."

"Don't let the judges see her now."

"Was PJ our first-round draft choice?"

"Some of these are for your homework, too, Mommy. You hafta cover them."

"Mine doesn't have a sticker on it."

"Why do I hafta answer Grandma's letter? She didn't ask me any questions."

"Mommy's in the closet with the telephone."

"Know why God makes twins? He gets tired of thinking up new faces."

"Daddy, are you home?"

"Smell them, PJ. They have a real good flavor."

"Grandma always says 'Well in MY day. . . .'
Isn't this still her day?"

"That's not a REAL sitter. It's our grandma. She
LIKES to take care of us."

"Mark Bennett chased me all over the playground, grabbed my hat, pulled my ponytail and socked my arm. I think he likes me."

"Mommy, turn on the burglar alarm and see if I can fool it."

"Most of the kids in our school have the same
ZIP code 'cept the last number
changes for some."

"You don't say 'he taked my chair' . . . it's 'my chair was tooken.'"

"I'm the doctor and Dolly's my answering service."

"This chicken is better than the Colonel's, Mommy. You oughta be a General!"

"Know what today is? October the oneth."

"Their mommies are gonna be mad. They're playin' in the mud."

"Can we come in the house yet?"

"Quit kickin' me, Billy, or Mommy will stop the car and you'll hafta get out and walk."

"If you drop it, it's called a fum-ball."

"I'm afraid this puzzle is too hard for you."
"Then could I do a soft one?"

"They have two bathrooms. Which one is for girls?"

"But four in the morning isn't the middle of the night."

"When summer gets finished here it goes to
South America."

"Why do they call him Bonnie Prince Charles? I thought that was a girl's name."

"Why is it always MY fault just because I'm the oldest?"

"Jeffy's not very brave, Mommy. He looks inside his sandwich before he eats it."

"We need it to put stripes on the field."

"See? We were only in there for five minutes."
"I didn't know it would take so soon."

"Grandma says hay is for horses!"

"We've been in this part already, Mommy. I
remember this vent."

"I was tired of getting kicked."

"You don't need to help me, Mommy. I can
undress it myself."

"You said our friend Mr. Tippit is part Indian. Do we know anybody who's part cowboy?"

"Mommy hung my plaster handprint in the
LIVIN' ROOM, not the recreation room!"

"This little pig went to market, this little pig stayed home, this. . . ."

"Daddy's family must have been poor when he was little. He only got 50 cents a week allowance."

"I think maybe I don't have enough candy in my blood."

"Can't we just go to a few houses tonight to get some practice?"

"Why do I always have to be what Billy was last year?"

"I'm making room for my candy and stuff so
Billy won't find 'em."

"There's nothin' on but grown-ups' programs
— talking heads."

"Why does grandma always call us by three or
four different names before she gets it right?"

"Jeffy learned that cough from me."

"Mommy! Now we can find out how good the
vacuum cleaner really is!"

"Daddy? Daddy? Daddy, why did you say I ask too many questions?"

"Is the tooth fairy married to the sandman?"

"All the other guys' moms are letting . . ."
"I am NOT all the other guys moms!"

"I've got an itchy trigger finger. I touched some poison ivy."

"Grandma baked some cookies but can't eat them all!"

"They're playin' patty-cake."

"Couldn't have been me, Mommy. Nobody has
taught me how to tangle yet!"

"Sure I can reach it. It's a piece of cake!"
"I thought it was a piece of pie."

"But I don't eat with the backs of them."

"Mommy! The toilet won't stop tinkling."

"That's only half a hug, Mommy. Use both arms."

"Miss Johnson was absent today. We had a
pretend teacher."

"Dolly's singin' 'Rudolph, the Red-Nosed Reindeer' and we haven't even had Thanksgiving yet!"

"Mommy, the sand is all downstairs now."

"Can I eat dinner over at Jason's? They're havin' hot dogs."

"Father Forrest said 'As you live, so shall you die.' I'll bet Billy dies in a messy room."

"Why do trees take their clothes off when it starts getting cold?"

You can have lots more fun
with
BIL KEANE and
THE FAMILY CIRCUS

30   Allow at least 4 weeks for delivery.   TA-60